PANAMA TF GUIDE FOR BEGINNERS

The Updated Concise Guide for Planning a Trip to Panama Including Top Destinations,Culture,Outdoor Adventures,Dining,Cuisine and Getting Around

Nicolash Enzo
Copyright@2023

TABLE OF CONTENT

CHAPTER 1

INTRODUCTION

Situated at the intersection of Central and South America, Panama is renowned for its remarkable natural landscapes, historical importance, and rich cultural variety. The short isthmus that serves as a connecting point between two continents has had a significant influence on the development of global commerce, providing a diverse variety of experiences that include both contemporary wonders and age-old traditions. Panama's diverse geography, characterized by its abundant rainforests, unspoiled beaches, and bustling metropolitan hubs, beckons tourists to go on a journey of discovery and delve into the riches it harbors.

The geographical and historical significance of this subject lies in its ability to connect continents and cultures.

Panama's geographical position as the isthmus between North and South America has bestowed upon it the epithet of the Crossroads of the World. This geographical phenomenon not only enabled the migration of animals across continents but also had a profound impact on the trajectory of human history. The Panama Canal, widely recognized as a remarkable achievement in engineering, serves as a vital link between the Atlantic and Pacific Oceans, facilitating uninterrupted marine trade routes and exerting a substantial influence on worldwide business.

In addition to its notable geographical importance, Panama has a rich historical heritage that is intricately interwoven with a wide range of cultural influences. For millennia, the regions in question have been inhabited by indigenous groups such as the Guna Yala and Emberá, predating the arrival of Christopher Columbus. These people have left a lasting heritage characterized by their rich customs, artistic expressions, and sustainable ways of life. The advent of European colonialism in the region introduced Spanish cultural elements, leading to the amalgamation of indigenous and colonial traditions, which is discernible in the architectural styles, culinary practices, and overall lifestyle of the nation.

Title: The Cultural Mosaic: Tracing its Ancient Origins to Contemporary Dynamism

The cultural fabric of Panama is comprised of several elements, symbolizing distinct aspects of its historical background. Indigenous communities persist in upholding their ancient customs, giving visitors an opportunity to get insight into their ceremonies, craftsmanship, and manner of existence. The Guna Yala community, located in the San Blas archipelago, serves as a prime example of the preservation of cultural traditions via their colourful textiles, known as molas, and their independent administration.

The enduring impact of colonialism is evident in the architectural and urban landscape of Casco Viejo, located in Panama City. This historic district has cobblestone lanes that meander through a collection of well-preserved colonial-period structures, including churches and plazas.

This setting offers visitors a unique opportunity to immerse themselves in a bygone age. The dichotomy seen between the old district and the contemporary skyline of the city serves as a visual representation of Panama's adeptness in achieving a harmonious coexistence between its historical heritage and its aspirations for the future.

Natural Splendors: Exploring the Biodiversity of Rainforests and Coral Reefs

The unique terrain of Panama offers a multitude of opportunities for anyone with a passion for nature to engage in recreational activities. Lush jungles, such as the Soberanía National Park, exhibit a profusion of diverse fauna, including species like as howler monkeys, toucans, and the enigmatic jaguar. Hiking trails such as the Sendero Los Quetzales provide hikers with the opportunity to cross cloud forests and get a glimpse of the magnificent quetzal bird.

Panama's turquoise waters provide a rich abundance of marine species, making it an enticing destination for anyone with a penchant for aquatic exploration. The archipelago of Bocas del Toro attracts snorkelers and divers due to its vivid coral reefs and diverse marine life. The Coiba National Park, designated as a UNESCO World Heritage Site, provides a protected marine environment that serves as a haven for the flourishing populations of hammerhead sharks and sea turtles. The San Blas Islands, characterized by their pristine seas and fine white dunes, provide a tranquil retreat.

Title: The Contemporary Pulse: Urban Centers and Innovation In recent times, urban centers have emerged as significant hubs for innovation and progress.

The city of Panama City serves as a prominent representation of Panama's contemporary state, showcasing a vibrant urban center that effectively harmonizes elements of both traditional and progressive aspects. Located centrally within the urban landscape, the Panama Canal serves as a prominent symbol of human intellect and aspiration. The Miraflores Visitor Center offers a full examination of the historical and operational aspects of the canal, providing visitors with the opportunity to see the remarkable transit of large vessels via the locks.

In the middle of the urban expansion, the Amador Causeway provides a tranquil respite, adorned with a variety of dining establishments, retail outlets, and awe-inspiring vistas of the Pacific Ocean. The urban landscape of the city, characterized by modern high-rise buildings, serves as a visual representation of Panama's growing prominence as a center for financial activities, commercial endeavors, and innovative developments.

Panama is a location that surpasses geographical limits and temporal limitations. The country's geographical features include a diverse range of landscapes, spanning from ethereal hills veiled in mist to picturesque beaches basking in the warmth of the sun. Its cultural heritage seamlessly integrates old wisdom with contemporary dynamism, while its historical narrative weaves together stories of both conflict and achievement. As individuals traverse the passageways of the Panama Canal, engage in the festivities of Carnaval, or engage in dialogue with indigenous craftsmen, they actively contribute to the complex tapestry that characterizes this remarkable country.

Panama has a diverse range of attractions that captivate tourists, including the exploration of lush rainforests, admiration of impressive architectural achievements, and interaction with communities who uphold traditional traditions. The nation in question exhibits a complex interplay between historical and contemporary elements, resulting in a multifaceted fabric that mirrors the diversity and abundance of the physical environment.

CHAPTER 2

Exploring Panama's Top Destinations

Panama, a country characterized by its dynamic contrasts and varied topography, entices tourists with a wide array of extraordinary locations that appeal to a broad range of interests and inclinations. Each place, ranging from the technological wonders of Panama City to the pristine beauty of the San Blas Islands, has its own narrative and provides a distinctive experiential encounter. This discourse aims to undertake an examination of Panama's prominent sites, whereby the convergence of history, culture, and environment gives rise to an indelible tapestry of discovery.

Panama City is a metropolis that serves as a convergence point between historical heritage and modern advancements.

Panama City, the focal point of Panama's urban appeal, represents a city that harmoniously amalgamates its historical allure with its modern vibrancy. The Panama Canal, which commands the city's skyline, stands as a remarkable tribute to the remarkable genius and unwavering tenacity of humanity. The Miraflores Visitor Center serves as an entrance to this remarkable feat of engineering, providing visitors with a comprehensive understanding of the canal's historical background, operational processes, and its importance in international commerce. As massive vessels go through the canal locks, onlookers see a display of meticulous coordination and formidable force that has significantly influenced the trajectory of global trade.

The historic area of Casco Viejo in Panama City offers visitors a nostalgic journey through time, characterized by its cobblestone alleys, buildings from the colonial period, and picturesque plazas. The designated UNESCO World Heritage Site serves as a dynamic medium that chronicles the historical accounts of Spanish colonialism, incursions by pirates, and the amalgamation of many cultures. Tourists have the opportunity to engage in the exploration of intricately designed cathedrals, such as the Metropolitan Cathedral, and partake in the consumption of regional culinary delights at vibrant street markets. During the sunset hours, Casco Viejo undergoes a notable metamorphosis, evolving into a dynamic center of nocturnal activities, characterized by the presence of music, dancing, and joviality that saturate the atmosphere.

Bocas del Toro: A Destination of Tropical Splendor and Aquatic Recreational Opportunities

The archipelago of Bocas del Toro offers a picturesque sanctuary characterized by its turquoise seas, pristine white sand beaches, and abundant rainforests, making it an ideal destination for anyone in search of a tranquil island getaway. This tropical destination provides a wide range of activities for those who are passionate about water-based pursuits and those who have a deep appreciation for the natural world. Snorkelers and divers are presented with an aquatic environment that showcases a plethora of brilliant coral reefs bustling with an array of unique marine species, such as parrotfish, seahorses, and vividly colored nudibranchs. The pristine waters of Starfish Beach entice tourists to luxuriate in the sunlight and observe the marine organisms that inhabit the shoreline, often known as starfish.

In addition to its coastal attractions, Bocas del Toro has opportunities for individuals to explore the adjacent jungles, which are home to a variety of wildlife such as howler monkeys, sloths, and toucans, thriving inside the lush vegetation. Experience the biological richness of the area by engaging in activities such as ziplining through the canopy or taking a boat trip through the mangroves. Located inside Bastimentos Island, the National Marine Park offers an unspoiled environment characterized by coral reefs and mangrove forests. This pristine area provides an opportunity for tourists to see and appreciate the intricate interplay between marine and terrestrial organisms.

Boquete, a region situated in the highlands of Panama, is renowned for its natural beauty and its status as a prominent hub for coffee production.

Located in the elevated regions of Panama, the town of Boquete presents an appealing contrast to the surrounding environment via its temperate weather, verdant terrain, and serene atmosphere. The region under consideration, which attracts those with an affinity for nature and those seeking tranquility, is primarily characterized by the imposing prominence of Volcan Baru, the highest summit in the nation. Hiking aficionados have the opportunity to undertake a demanding expedition to reach the peak, where their arduous efforts are met with a captivating dawn that offers expansive vistas of the Pacific and Atlantic Oceans.

The importance of Boquete goes beyond its aesthetic appeal, as it serves as the central hub for Panama's prosperous coffee industry. The mountains are adorned with coffee farms, which beckon tourists to explore the complicated processes involved in cultivating, harvesting, and roasting coffee. The guided tours offered at the farms give an immersive educational experience that delves into the intricate process of coffee manufacturing. These excursions provide a sensory trip, allowing participants to see the whole journey from the cultivation of coffee beans to the final result in a cup.

The San Blas Islands are renowned for their indigenous culture and pristine beauty.

The San Blas Islands, situated as an archipelago along the northeastern coast of Panama, provide a unique prospect for individuals to deeply engage with the vibrant culture of the Guna Yala people, all the while enjoying the pristine allure of the Caribbean region. The establishment of this autonomous indigenous area serves as evidence of the Guna Yala community's dedication to the preservation of their cultural practices and natural resources. The islands' azure seas, pristine white beaches, and gently swinging coconut palms provide a gorgeous setting conducive to both leisure and discovery.

A trip to the San Blas Islands offers an opportunity to get an understanding of the traditions, customs, and creative expression of the Guna Yala community. Molas, which are meticulously crafted fabrics portraying narratives from Guna mythology and everyday life, serve as both vivid artistic expressions and significant cultural artifacts. Tourists get the opportunity to interact with the Guna Yala community, actively participate in their cultural ceremonies, and acquire knowledge about their enduring sustainable traditions, which have effectively safeguarded their islands for several generations.

In conclusion, Panama offers a diverse range of experiences that might be likened to a kaleidoscope.

The premier attractions in Panama provide a vibrant portrayal of a nation that commemorates its historical heritage, embraces its contemporary state, and eagerly anticipates its next developments.

With its vibrant urban environment and pristine natural landscapes, Panama City and the San Blas Islands provide unique combinations of historical significance, cultural richness, and awe-inspiring natural wonders. Panama offers a range of captivating experiences for travelers, encompassing the awe-inspiring engineering feat of the Panama Canal, the vibrant coral reefs of Bocas del Toro, the scenic highlands of Boquete, and the opportunity to engage with indigenous communities in the San Blas Islands. These diverse attractions invite individuals to embark on a journey of exploration, one that embraces the rich tapestry of both human and natural wonders that characterize this extraordinary country.

CHAPTER 3

Cultural Experiences

The cultural environment of Panama is characterized by a diverse amalgamation of indigenous history, colonial legacy, and contemporary influences. As individuals participate in the exploration of the nation's dynamic communities and immerse themselves in their longstanding customs, they embark on a riveting voyage through historical eras and cultural heritage. The cultural experiences in Panama include a range of interesting customs observed by indigenous communities, as well as the exuberant festivals celebrated across the country. These experiences provide an immersive and illuminating opportunity for individuals to get a better grasp of the nation's essence.

Indigenous communities play a vital role as custodians of ancestral wisdom.

For millennia, Indigenous groups in Panama have flourished, diligently safeguarding their cultural practices and accumulated knowledge over successive generations. Within the several groups under consideration, it is evident that the Guna Yala people exhibit remarkable endurance and a strong sense of cultural pride. The San Blas Islands provide tourists a unique chance to engage with the Guna Yala community and get a deeper understanding of their everyday existence, creative manifestations, and comprehensive perspective on the world.

The elaborate molas of the Guna Yala community are highly regarded for their ability to visually depict their beliefs and tales via colourful fabrics. The depicted scenes from nature, mythology, and tradition are skillfully constructed masterpieces, using reverse appliqué methods. Interacting with craftsmen from the Guna Yala community provides an opportunity not only to admire their artistic skills but also to get a deeper understanding of the profound meaning embedded within each design.

The Emberá villages, which are located in the jungles of Panama, provide a comprehensive and immersive perspective into their unique cultural practices and way of life. Visitors are cordially welcomed, encouraged to engage in their routine undertakings, and acquainted with their customary musical, choreographic, and culinary practices. The Emberá people engage in the creation of visually striking body painting, using natural colours, which serves as a significant cultural practice denoting a rite of passage and functioning as a visual manifestation of their cultural heritage.

Title: Festivals and Events: Commemorating Life and Cultural Heritage
Introduction: Festivals and events play a significant role in commemorating life and preserving cultural heritage. These occasions provide communities with an opportunity to come together, celebrate, and showcase their unique traditions and customs. This article explores the importance of festivals and events

The calendar of Panama is marked by a multitude of lively festivals and events, each serving as a commemoration of the country's unique cultural legacy and energetic energy. Carnaval, regarded as the most extravagant of these festivities, has the remarkable ability to metamorphose towns into vibrant spectacles of vivid hues, melodious tunes, and rhythmic movements. Carnaval, which takes place in the week before Lent, serves as a manifestation of Panama's amalgamation of Spanish, African, and indigenous cultural elements. Dancers with intricate costumes, colorful masks, and meticulously designed floats go in a procession down the thoroughfares, extending an invitation to onlookers to partake in the festivities.

The Panamanian population, characterized by a strong religious devotion, attaches great importance to Semana Santa, often known as Holy Week. Various communities around the nation participate in processions, reenactments, and rituals that serve as commemorative acts to honor the Passion of Christ. The urban thoroughfares become animated with somber but evocative exhibitions of religious belief and dedication, engendering a spiritual ambiance that deeply affects both residents and tourists.

Independence Day, observed on November 3rd, is an additional event that exemplifies the deep-seated patriotic enthusiasm in Panama. In observance of its political detachment from Colombia in the year 1903, this occasion is distinguished via the organization of processions, musical performances, and pyrotechnic displays. The auditory landscape of the streets reverberates with the melodic strains of traditional music, while the celestial expanse above is adorned with a vibrant array of hues, therefore cultivating a collective sentiment of cohesion and admiration.

Exploring Culinary Traditions: An Academic Exploration of Gastronomy

The culinary landscape of Panama is a manifestation of its rich historical and geographical diversity. Panamanian culinary traditions include a harmonious amalgamation of indigenous, Spanish, Afro-Caribbean, and Latin American elements, yielding a captivating amalgam of gustatory and olfactory sensations.

Sancocho, a robust chicken stew, is often regarded as a culinary symbol of Panama. This recipe exemplifies the agricultural riches of the nation, using ingredients such as yucca, plantains, maize, and several other vegetables. The act of partaking in a communal meal is often embraced and valued within the cultural context of Panama, serving as a symbolic representation of the significance attributed to unity and the act of sharing.

Ceviche, a culinary preparation consisting of freshly sourced fish marinated in lime juice and a blend of spices, serves as a representation of Panama's rich coastal history. Ceviche, regardless of the seafood used, has a tangy and invigorating flavor that showcases the many offerings of the ocean. When served over crispy plantains or saltine crackers, this meal serves as a good example of how basic components can be elevated into refined delicacies.

Arroz with Pollo, a much cherished culinary dish in Panamanian families, consists of a harmonious blend of rice and chicken, offering a source of comfort and satisfaction. This recipe exemplifies a combination of Spanish influence with the use of locally sourced ingredients, as it incorporates saffron, veggies, and other flavors. Arroz with pollo, accompanied by fried ripe plantains, embodies the fundamental characteristics of Panamanian cuisine, characterized by its opulent flavors and deep-rooted cultural heritage.

Preservation of Traditions: An Ethical and Respectful Approach to Exploration

When engaging with the varied cultural experiences in Panama, it is crucial for tourists to approach each contact with respect, curiosity, and awareness. Engagement with indigenous people should be conducted in manners that demonstrate respect for their autonomy and preservation of their cultural heritage. It is recommended to give precedence to guided tours and community-led projects that effectively enhance the economic and ethical empowerment of these communities.

When engaging in festivals and events, it is important to demonstrate reverence for the customs and traditions of the local community. It is crucial to acknowledge that these festivities are profoundly ingrained in spiritual ideologies and historical narratives. Engaging in non-intrusive observation and obtaining permission prior to capturing images may foster a mutually beneficial and considerate encounter for both tourists and residents.

In the realm of gastronomic investigations, patronizing local restaurants and street sellers not only affords individuals the opportunity to indulge in genuine tastes, but also plays a crucial role in bolstering the economic well-being of nearby communities. By actively interacting with vendors, inquiring about the constituents of their products, and expressing gratitude for their expertise, individuals may establish significant relationships and foster a reciprocal trade.

The cultural experiences in Panama include a rich tapestry that is intricately woven with elements of tradition, creativity, and interpersonal connections. By actively engaging with indigenous people, actively participating in festivals, appreciating traditional cuisine, and treating every interaction with respect, tourists embark on a transformative experience that goes beyond mere tourism. It becomes an enriching voyage of cultural immersion and deep knowledge. As individuals in Panama generously express their emotions and recount their own experiences, tourists are included into a story that transcends national boundaries and celebrates the inherent value of multiculturalism.

CHAPTER 4

Outdoor Adventures

Panama, a nation characterized by its abundant natural beauty and diverse geographical features, entices adventurous explorers to immerse themselves in the vast expanse of the outdoors. Panama, renowned for its varied ecosystems, majestic mountains, and unspoiled waterways, is an enticing prospect for those passionate about outdoor activities, providing an exhilarating respite from the mundane. The country's outdoor activities include traveling forest paths and exploring vivid coral reefs, offering individuals an opportunity to go on a voyage of exploration, experience adrenaline-inducing moments, and establish a deep connection with the natural environment.

Hiking and nature trails provide an opportunity to uncover the hidden secrets of the rainforest.

The rainforests of Panama possess abundant vegetation and serve as a habitat for several fascinating phenomena that are yet to be discovered. The nation offers a diverse selection of hiking paths that accommodate individuals of all levels of experience, ensuring opportunities to see elusive fauna, discover concealed waterfalls, and appreciate expansive scenic views.

Sendero Los Quetzales is well recognized as a prominent path, offering a captivating expedition through the cloud woods of Boquete. The route, which derives its name from the magnificent quetzal bird, meanders through ethereal terrains, providing intermittent views of vibrant orchids, majestic trees, and secretive fauna. Hikers have the potential to see the quetzal's vibrant and shimmering feathers, an occurrence that epitomizes the captivating allure of Panama's untamed natural environment.

Within the confines of Soberanía National Park, the Pipeline Road provides a unique chance for observers to watch the remarkable diversity of bird species that inhabit the area. With a diverse array of avian inhabitants, including more than 500 distinct species such as toucans, parrots, and harpy eagles, this particular route provides an auditory experience characterized by a harmonious chorus of birdcalls, as individuals leisurely navigate through the lush and vibrant uppermost layer of foliage. The rainforest's environment exhibits a vivid display of life, whereby each footstep reveals the animated presence of butterflies in flight and monkeys traversing the above branches.

Water-based Adventures: Exploring the Aquatic Realm

The waters of Panama are renowned for their exceptional quality, offering a remarkable aquatic ecosystem that entices people to engage in a variety of activities such as diving, snorkeling, surfing, and kayaking. These habitats are globally recognized for their compelling and awe-inspiring characteristics.

Coiba National Park, designated as a UNESCO World Heritage Site, attracts the attention of diving and snorkeling enthusiasts, inviting them to delve into its submerged domain. Abundant with a diverse array of marine organisms and thriving coral ecosystems, these aquatic environments provide as a protected habitat for many species including hammerhead sharks, manta rays, and sea turtles. Upon submerging into the depths of the ocean, divers are met with a vibrant array of hues and intricate formations, evoking a captivating visual spectacle.

Santa Catalina provides a favorable environment for those passionate about surfing, characterized by reliable wave conditions and a relaxed ambiance. The surf breakers at this location are suitable for surfers of many ability levels, ranging from beginners to experienced individuals. Surfers encounter a profound sensation of liberation and intense excitement as they navigate the peaks of the Pacific Ocean's undulating waves. This unique experience is only facilitated by the vastness and dynamism of the oceanic environment.

Kayaking serves as a serene method for exploring the coastal and river landscapes of Panama. The Chiriquí Gulf National Marine Park provides a serene aquatic environment characterized by tranquil seas, flourishing mangrove forests, and a collection of petite islands that provide ideal conditions for engaging in kayaking trips. Paddlers provide the ability to go through constricted aquatic passages, so facilitating the opportunity to see a wide array of avian species and perhaps engage with dolphins that exhibit playful behavior while swimming in close proximity.

Mountain Adventures: The Pursuit of Summiting Peaks and Overcoming Altitudes

Panama's mountainous regions provide an ideal environment for anyone seeking exhilarating experiences at high elevations and captivating vistas.

The Volcan Baru, which stands as the highest summit in the nation, entices hikers to undertake its ascent in order to see a dawn that reveals the presence of two vast bodies of water—the Pacific and the Atlantic—when the weather is clear. Despite the difficulties encountered throughout the walk, it provides a profound feeling of achievement and a breathtaking panorama that makes each stride meaningful.

In addition to engaging in outdoor activities, the verdant mountains of Panama provide an idyllic setting for those with a passion for zip-lining. Boquete, renowned for its canopy tours, provides an exhilarating experience as individuals go over the uppermost branches of trees, catching sight of toucans and butterflies in mid-flight underneath them. The amalgamation of velocity, elevation, and inherent aesthetic appeal engenders an indelible encounter that deeply connects with one's innate inclination for exploration.

Respecting Nature: An Examination of Ethical and Sustainable Approaches to Adventuring

When engaging in outdoor activities in Panama, it is important to approach them with a strong emphasis on environmental conservation and the well-being of local populations. By adhering to the principles of Leave No Trace, one may assure the preservation of the natural beauty that is now being enjoyed, so safeguarding it for the benefit of future generations. It is essential to adhere to trail markers and designated locations in order to mitigate ecological effect and save vulnerable ecosystems.

Participate in endeavors that promote the growth of local economies and the advancement of ecotourism efforts. A significant number of outdoor excursions and guides are facilitated by individuals who are indigenous to the area and possess extensive expertise about the ecosystems present in the region. By selecting these alternatives, individuals not only make a positive contribution towards sustainable development but also get valuable perspectives from individuals who possess a deep affinity with the environment.

The outdoor experiences in Panama exemplify the ethos of exploration, motivating individuals to explore beyond their familiar boundaries and appreciate the untamed splendor of the natural world. Engaging in various activities such as trekking through jungles, exploring marine wonderlands, conquering mountain summits, or participating in responsible ecotourism endeavors serves to strengthen the bond between mankind and the natural world. When individuals engage in the exploration of Panama's many landscapes, they are not just embarking upon a physical endeavor, but also embarking onto a transformative experience of self-discovery and a deepened awareness for the remarkable natural phenomena that exist within the outer environment.

CHAPTER 5

Cuisine and Dining

Located in the core of Panama's cultural amalgamation, there exists a gastronomic panorama that mirrors the country's multifaceted background and bountiful natural resources. Panama's culinary landscape encompasses a diverse array of gustatory experiences, ranging from vibrant street markets teeming with activity to refined dining establishments exuding elegance. This gastronomic tapestry showcases a captivating amalgamation of tastes, fragrances, and tactile sensations that serve as a narrative of the nation's historical, geographical, and cultural amalgamation. Engaging in a gastronomic exploration in Panama entails more than just gustatory gratification; it is immersing oneself in a multifaceted fabric of customs, ingenuity, and the appreciation of existence.

A Comprehensive Examination of Influences: Tracing the Evolution from Indigenous Origins to Colonial Legacies

The culinary legacy of Panama is intricately intertwined with the historical relationships of indigenous people, Spanish colonists, African slaves, and other immigrant groups. The amalgamation of many influences has engendered a distinctive gastronomic character that encompasses a diverse range of cultural heritages, culminating in culinary creations that are both recognizable and unexpected.

Sancocho, a robust chicken stew, is regarded as a distinctive Panamanian culinary creation that serves as a prime example of the nation's rich agricultural variety. The use of ingredients such as yucca, plantains, maize, and other vegetables in sancocho results in a culinary experience that encapsulates a rich tapestry of aromas and textures, deeply rooted in the historical context of the region. Frequently associated with social gatherings and ceremonial events, this culinary creation exemplifies the cordiality and conviviality that Panamanians graciously provide to their visitors.

Ceviche, a culinary preparation involving the marination of fresh fish in lime juice and a blend of spices, serves as a notable manifestation of Panama's coastal influences. This culinary preparation, which has a significant position in the gastronomy of several Latin American nations, showcases the influence of the country's geographical closeness to the ocean and its strong commitment to using fresh ingredients. Ceviche, whether prepared with fish, shrimp, or a combination of seafood, encapsulates the inherent coastal allure of Panama via its invigorating flavors.

Street Food and Markets: An Exquisite Culinary Experience

To experience the genuine flavors of Panama's gastronomic landscape, individuals should direct their attention to the vibrant street markets where the air is filled with the enticing scents of sizzling meats, fried plantains, and fragrant spices. The markets in question serve as more than just venues for dining; they provide insights into the daily experiences of Panamanian individuals, where discussions are exchanged as effortlessly as the aromatic smoke emanating from the grills.

Street food carts provide a wide variety of deep-fried delicacies, including empanadas, patacones (fried plantains), and carimañolas (cassava turnovers), presented in generous portions. These portable food items embody the amalgamation of native and colonial gastronomic traditions, delivering a rush of taste that is ideal for a convenient snack or an informal dinner while in transit.

Seaside Bounty: An Exhibition of Unspoiled Produce

Panama's culinary landscape is enriched by the presence of both the Pacific Ocean and the Caribbean Sea, which contribute significantly to the country's seafood options. Seafood enthusiasts will encounter an abundance of options, as they explore a diverse range of culinary creations that skillfully highlight the vast offerings of the ocean in both inventive and delightful ways.

The fusion of rice and fish is often used in the culinary realm to produce delectable dishes that embody the coastal culture of Panama. Arroz with camarones, a meal consisting of rice and shrimp, and arroz con mariscos, a dish comprising rice and mixed seafood, exemplify the intrinsic allure of Panama's coastal culture. The rice, imbued with the aromatic essence of saffron and a blend of spices, provides a foundation for the delectable marine delicacies, resulting in a cohesive amalgamation of tastes and mouthfeel.

Coffee and Sweet Delights: An Exploration of Culinary Excellence

Panama, renowned for its superior coffee beans, presents an exceptional coffee experience that beyond conventional drinking. The highlands are adorned with coffee farms, offering tourists the chance to engage in the practice of cultivating, harvesting, and roasting coffee. The guided tours provided at these estates provide a multisensory experience, taking visitors on a captivating trip through the verdant coffee fields and into the fragrant roasting rooms. These excursions shed light on the intricate process of transforming coffee beans into a delightful cup of coffee.

The confectionery and dessert offerings of Panama exemplify the nation's affinity for tropical fruits and native constituents. Ripe plantains undergo a culinary transformation to produce delectable confections such as tajadas, which are caramelized slices of plantains that exhibit a harmonious interplay of sweetness and texture. Cocadas, which are chewy confections made from coconut, serve as a tribute to the many coconut trees found in the region. On the other hand, raspados are icy delights that consist of shaved ice generously soaked in vibrant fruit syrups, offering a revitalizing escape from the warm climate of the tropics.

Dining Etiquette and Cultural Respect: The Significance of Sharing a Meal In this article, we will explore the importance of dining etiquette and cultural respect when it comes to the act of sharing a meal.

When embarking on a gastronomic exploration in Panama, it is important to bear in mind that eating experiences extend beyond just sustenance. They provide valuable opportunities for interpersonal connections and cultural immersion. In the context of eating in traditional settings or interacting with local people, it is of utmost importance to demonstrate respect and mindfulness towards local traditions.

Panamanian culture places a significant premium on the values of hospitality and communal sharing, hence necessitating one's preparedness to encounter ample servings and heartfelt gestures. In social contexts, it is customary for meals to be served in a family-style manner, fostering a shared feeling of camaraderie and unity among everyone. Embrace the cultural practice at hand and get pleasure from the communal act of sharing a meal with other individuals.

It is important to adhere to local eating etiquette as well. Regardless of the dining environment, it is important to adhere to proper etiquette by using utensils correctly and consuming food with the right hand. It is worth noting that the left hand is often designated for personal hygiene purposes. Exhibiting deference for indigenous cultures not only enhances one's personal encounter but also cultivates substantial interpersonal relationships with the individuals encountered.

Undertaking a gastronomic discovery in Panama represents a multisensory voyage, including the examination of tastes, smells, and textures that resonate with the country's historical, cultural, and geographical aspects. Every culinary creation has a narrative yearning to be relished, serving as a tribute to the innovative amalgamation of elements that shape Panama's gastronomic character. Panama's gastronomic world offers a diverse array of culinary experiences that reflect the country's indigenous origins, coastal appeal, and cultural relevance. From the traditional sancocho dish to the renowned ceviche and the ubiquitous presence of coffee, each mouthful serves as an opportunity to fully engage with the vivid spirit of Panama's culinary heritage. While exploring street markets, indulging in coastal delicacies, and engaging in communal dining experiences, one will discern that the intrinsic nature of Panama's cultural identity permeates each culinary creation. This harmonious amalgamation of flavors evokes profound sensations and imparts an enduring impression on the gastronomic expedition undertaken.

THE END

Printed in Great Britain
by Amazon

37564544R00036